SAVING THE WHOOPING CRANE

BY
SUSAN E. GOODMAN

ILLUSTRATED BY
PHYLLIS V. SAROFF

M Millbrook Press/Minneapolis

Millbrook Press
A division of Lerner Publishing Group, Inc.
241 First Avenue North
Minneapolis, MN 55401 U.S.A

Website address: www.lernerbooks.com

Library of Congress Cataloging-in-Publication Data

Goodman, Susan E., 1952-
    Saving the whooping crane / by Susan E. Goodman ; illustrations by Phyllis V.
Saroff.
        p.   cm. — (On my own science)
    ISBN 978–0–8225–6748–6 (lib. bdg. : alk. paper)
    1. Whooping crane—Juvenile literature. I. Saroff, Phyllis V., ill. II. Title.
QL696.G84G66 2008
598.3—dc22   2006039577
Manufactured in the United States of America
2 3 4 5 6 7 – JR – 13 12 11 10 09 08

To Zach—my second, third,
and fourth wind
—S. E. G.

For Doris
—P. V. S.

A New Beginning

Whooping cranes have lived on the earth
for 65 million years.
These birds lived all over North America.
Then farmers took the cranes' land.
People hunted them for their feathers.
By the 1940s, only 15 whoopers were left.
This tiny flock lived
in the western United States.

People worked hard to help the cranes.
The flock grew to 200 birds.
But having only one flock was dangerous.
A storm or disease could wipe them all out.
Two wild flocks living in different areas
would be much safer.
But how do you start a new flock
of whooping cranes?

Scientists needed whooping crane chicks
to form a new flock.
They couldn't just move adult whoopers
to a new spot.
Whooping cranes migrate.
They live up north in summer,
then fly south to spend the winter
in warmer weather.
Each spring, whoopers return to the place
where they learned to fly.
Adult birds won't accept a new home.

The western flock of whoopers
lived in Canada in the summer.
They went to Texas in the winter.
Scientists wanted the new flock
to live in the East.
They would spend summers in Necedah,
Wisconsin, and winters in Florida,
as other whoopers did long ago.

The scientists decided to
hatch crane eggs
and raise the chicks themselves.
But the scientists wanted the chicks
to grow up to be wild.
They couldn't get used to humans.
So the scientists would pretend
to be whooping cranes.
White costumes would hide their bodies.
Hoods would cover their faces.
Each would wear a crane puppet
on one arm.
They would never speak near the chicks.
Instead, they would play tapes
of crane parents calling to their young.

Operation Migration

Tap, tap, tap.

The egg was one month old.

It was time for the chick inside to hatch.

The tiny whooping crane finally
broke through the shell.

He wiggled out, wet and tired.

He saw a black beak, gold eyes,
and a patch of red.

Mom!

The chick cuddled close.
From then on,
he would accept no other mother.
He had no idea that his mother
was a puppet on a scientist's arm.
This chick was the first member
of the new flock of whooping cranes.
Ten other chicks would also hatch.

The scientists used their puppets
to teach the chicks how whooping cranes live.
They showed the chicks how to eat and drink.
They taught them where to sleep.
They even broke up fights between chicks.
The scientists also kept some adult
whoopers nearby.
The chicks needed to know what real
adult whooping cranes looked like.

In the wild, chicks follow their parents.

They run, flapping their wings to keep up.

In time, this is how the chicks learn to fly.

But puppet parents cannot fly.

How were these chicks going to learn?

Flight School

Scientists used an ultralight plane
to teach the young cranes to fly.
The chicks were used to the engine's roar.
They had heard it while they were still
inside their eggs.
But they had to learn to follow the plane.
The scientist who was flying the plane
used a special puppet to teach them.
The puppet played a crane call
that made the chicks want to follow it.

When the chicks followed the plane,

the puppet gave them treats.

At first, the chicks walked behind the plane.

Then the plane went faster.

The chicks did too, flapping all the while.

Each day, their muscles got stronger.

Their feathers grew longer.

At two months old, they were big and strong.

They ran and flapped,

and suddenly they were flying!

On the first few flights,

the chicks followed the plane back home.

But one day,

they landed in a nearby marsh instead.

Their caretakers wanted the chicks

to fly home.

One man went to the marsh.

He covered himself with a tarp.

He became the Swamp Monster!

The next time the cranes

flew near the marsh,

Swamp Monster flapped his scary arms.

The birds decided to follow the plane

after all!

The cranes practiced flying
almost every day.
Fall was coming.
Soon the plane would
lead them to Florida.
They had to be strong enough
to fly 1,250 miles.
They had to learn to recognize
their Wisconsin home from high in the air.
When they returned in the spring,
they would have to find it on their own!

Up, Up, and Away!

On October 17, 2001,
the whoopers began their journey.
Two of the eleven chicks had gotten sick
and died.
Another couldn't fly well
and was moved to a zoo.
One ultralight led eight birds toward Florida.
Another plane led any wandering cranes
back to the group.
On the very first day,
one whooper went his own way.
The crew got him back.
But they were afraid that he might
lead other cranes off course.
That bird ended up riding in a truck
for a while instead of flying!

Sometimes the cranes flew in a V pattern
behind the ultralight.
Flying this way helped them save energy.
They could coast on the wind
coming off the plane's wings.
As they migrated,
the whoopers needed places to eat and sleep.
The scientists had picked rest stops for them.
Each day, a crew drove to the next rest site.
They set up a pen for the birds
and trailers for the people.
They rushed to finish
before the cranes arrived.
They didn't want the cranes to see them.

The cranes had some good days,
but there were bad ones too.
One night,
a huge storm tore their pen to bits.
Only three whoopers stayed near the ruins.
The crew grabbed their crane costumes.
They searched through the rain
and lightning.
They played crane calls and listened
for the missing whoopers' answering cries.

By 2:30 A.M.,
they had found all of the cranes but one.
The next morning,
they discovered his body.
He had flown into a power line and died.
Everyone was awfully sad.
The first 10 days of the trip
had been very hard.
The group had gone less than 100 miles.
They had more than 1,000 miles to go.

Florida Bound

The flock's luck changed the very next day.
Light, steady wind helped the cranes fly.
They traveled 95 miles before landing.
The whoopers flew that far a few days.
But other days,
the wind blew the wrong way.
Then the cranes had to wait
before going on.
One time, the flock had to battle
strong winds to fly over a big hill.
One whooper turned back and got lost.

Luckily, the scientists had put a leg band
on each bird before the trip.
The bands put out radio signals.
Scientists could find the lost crane
by following his band's signal.
The next morning, the scientists learned
that the crane was near a river.
They rushed through the forest,
playing their crane call.
The lost whooper answered from the air.
But there were too many trees
for him to land safely.
One crew member saw a bare hilltop.
He ran hard toward the hill,
playing the call over and over.
The whooper landed right beside him.
After a night alone, the bird was glad
to see the familiar white costume.

Soon the cranes were
traveling together again.
Farther south,
the weather was warm.
Flying is hard exercise in
warm weather.
So the cranes had to fly
shorter distances each day.

Fifty days after starting the trip, the group
finally flew over their new home in Florida.
The pilot of the ultralight
turned off his crane call.
A caretaker on the ground began
playing the call so the cranes would land.
And that was exactly what
the whoopers did.

Winter in Florida

Over the winter,

the whoopers explored their new home.

Most of the time, they stayed in their pen.

It was so big that it had a pond inside it.

A puppet parent showed them

how to peck apart tasty crabs.

A dummy in the pond kept them company.

It encouraged the birds to stay in the water.

That was the safest place for them to sleep.

That way, they could hear splashing

if a predator came near.

Even so, two birds did not survive.

They were killed by bobcats.

The new flock was down to five birds.

Their caretakers called them

the Florida Five.

People checked on the whoopers every day.

But they stayed hidden.

The cranes needed to think

that they were on their own.

Spring came.

Whooping cranes and other migratory birds
eat more in the spring.

They gain extra weight that will provide
energy for their long flight north.

Then, when the days are long enough,
they leave.

But what about the Florida Five?

Would the whoopers know when to leave?

On April 9, the sun was shining.

The wind blew from south to north.

Suddenly, radio signals told the caretakers

that the whoopers were flying!

The birds were riding the wind.

They were moving FAST.

Two caretakers jumped into their trucks.

They rushed to the highway.

There were 1,250 miles to go!

Would all five cranes make it

to Wisconsin?

Going North

The spring migration
was a very different trip.
The flock could go much faster
without the ultralights.

Unlike planes, birds can ride thermals.

Thermals are currents
caused by rising warm air.

Birds ride them the way surfers ride waves.

That first day,
the whoopers traveled 217 miles!

A few days later, one crane flew off.

This time, there was no plane to follow her.

A caretaker drove off in a truck

to track the bird.

At the end of the day,

this whooper had flown 144 miles.

The other four had traveled 200 miles.

Soon these cranes reached Lake Michigan.

They started to circle.

They didn't know which way to go!

If they turned east, they would be

on the wrong side of a huge lake.

But after two hours of circling,

they finally turned west!

That night, they found a marsh

inside the city of Chicago.

The fifth crane landed

in the nearby state of Indiana.

Eleven days after they left Florida,
four whoopers flew into Necedah.
They landed near the pen
where they had been raised.
The fifth whooper was in a marsh
with some sandhill cranes.
Sandhill cranes are relatives
of whooping cranes.
Two weeks later,
she finally made her way to Necedah.

The migration was a success.
All five whoopers had found
their way home.
The Florida Five were the first
whooping cranes to migrate to Wisconsin
in more than 100 years.

Whooper Update

In 2002, the Florida Five
migrated on their own,
while ultralights led 16 new cranes south.
Each year, the flock got bigger.
By 2006, the flock had more than 80 birds.
The whoopers had started
having chicks of their own.
The adults will teach their chicks
how to fly to Florida.
And the whooping crane flock
will keep on growing.

Afterword

Many organizations worked together to help bring back the whooping cranes. You can learn more about the project by visiting these websites.

Journey North
www.learner.org/jnorth

Operation Migration
www.operationmigration.org

Whooping Crane Eastern Partnership
www.bringbackthecranes.org

The founders of Operation Migration were the first humans to fly with birds. In their first project, they used ultralight planes to lead a small flock of Canada geese from Ontario, Canada, to the state of Virginia. This story inspired the movie *Fly Away Home*. Operation Migration has published several books and documentary videos about their work.

Glossary

chick (CHIHK): a baby whooping crane

flock (FLAHK): a group of birds

marsh (MAHRSH): low land that is wet and soft

migrate (MY-grayt): to move from one place to another when the season changes

predator (PREH-duh-tuhr): an animal that hunts and eats other animals

thermals (THUR-muhlz): currents caused by rising warm air

ultralight plane (UHL-truh-lyt PLAYN): a small, lightweight, slow-flying airplane

Learn More about Whooping Cranes and Migration

Cone, Molly. *Come Back, Salmon*. San Francisco: Sierra Club Books for Children, 1992.

Duden, Jane. *Whoop Dreams: The Historic Migration*. Logan, IA: Perfection Learning Corporation, 2004.

DuTemple, Lesley A. *North American Cranes*. Minneapolis: Carolrhoda Books, Inc., 1999.

Lishman, Bill, and Joe Duff. *Hope Takes Wing: A Journey to Save a Species*. VHS. Stevens Point, WI: Solterra Productions, 2005.

Parker, Janice. *Whooping Cranes*. Chicago: Raintree, 1997.

Patent, Dorothy Hinshaw. *The Whooping Crane: A Comeback Story*. New York: Clarion Books, 1988.

Rylant, Cynthia. *The Journey: Stories of Migration*. New York: Blue Sky Press, 2006.

Simon, Seymour. *Ride the Wind: Airborne Journeys of Animals and Plants*. San Diego: Browndeer Press, 1997.